MATHS PRACTICE PAPERS

FOR SENIOR SCHOOL ENTRY

ANSWERS AND EXPLANATIONS

PETER ROBSON

 **Newby Books**

This book contains answers and explanations relating to questions in
'Maths Practice Papers for Senior School Entry' (ISBN 978-1-872686-39-4)

ISBN 978-1-872686-40-0

NEWBY BOOKS
Easingwold Town Hall Company Ltd
The Advertiser Office, Market Place
Easingwold, York YO61 3AB
www.newbybooks.co.uk

Printed by G. H. Smith & Son, Easingwold, York YO61 3AB
Telephone 01347 821329. Facsimile 01347 822576
www.ghsmith.com

PAPER A. Answers and explanations.

1. 1111

2. 555

3. 8448

$$\begin{array}{r} 1\,9\,2 \\ \times \quad 4\,4 \\ \hline 7\,6\,8 \\ 7\,6\,8\,\mathbf{0} \\ \hline 8\,4\,4\,8 \end{array}$$

4. 666   74% of 100 = 74,   so 74% of 900 = 9 × 74 = 666

5. 305 035   There are no hundreds   so answer is 305 035

6. £188   £3 760 ÷ 20   is equivalent to £376 ÷ 2 = £188

7. 26·266   Columns are important. Write the decimal points first, in a straight column . Then write the numbers.

$$\begin{array}{r} 1\,6\cdot 1\,7 \\ +\; 6\cdot 0\,9\,6 \\ 4\cdot 0 \\ \hline \end{array}$$

8. 1.25 p.m. $\frac{3}{4}$ hour = 45 min.   3 hours after 9.40 a.m. is 12.40 p.m.
         45 min after 12.40 is 1.25 p.m.

9. 26   Add all the sweets together and divide by 2 = 49 which makes both sides equal. So 49 – 23 = 26 sweets must be moved. So left side is 75 – 26 = 49, right side is 23 + 26 = 49.

10. 2·2, 28%, 0.23, $\frac{1}{5}$, 0.027   Change any non-decimals into decimals.

0.23	=	0·23
2·2	=	2·2
28%	=	0·28
$\frac{1}{5}$	=	0·2
0.027	=	0·027

11. (a) 963
(b) 396   Even numbers end with 0, 2, 4, 6 or 8.
(c) 693   Best done by trying them all until you spot the correct one.

12. (a) 6, –6   Subtracting 12 each time.
(b) 81, 243   Multiplying by 3 each time.

13. (a) £7.33   Work in pounds, remembering that 92p = £0.92 and 99p = £0.99
(b) £2.67   For subtracting, call £10.00 'nine pounds ninety ten'

$$\begin{array}{r} 9\,.\,9\,10 \\ -\; 7\,.\,3\,3 \\ \hline \end{array}$$

    _or_ say £7.33 + **2p** = £7.35 . Then £7.35 + **5p** = £7.40 . £7.40 + **10p** = £7.50 .
    £7.50 + **50p** = £8.00   Then £8.00 + **£2** = £10.00. Then add all the bits of change.

14. 32 cm   Area of rectangle = length × width. So width is 63 ÷ 9 = 7 cm
         Perimeter is   9 + 7 + 9 + 7 = 32 cm

15. (a) $\frac{1}{3}$ There are 12 squares. 4 are shaded. Fraction shaded is $\frac{4}{12}$ = (dividing both numerator and denominator by 4) $= \frac{1}{3}$

    (b) 5   If $\frac{1}{4}$ remains unshaded, $\frac{3}{4}$ must be shaded . $\frac{3}{4} = \frac{9}{12}$ so 5 more must be shaded.

16. (a) Mercury   A 'thermometer line' may be helpful.

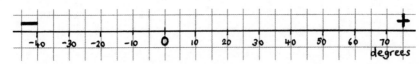

(b) 103°C $-39 + 39 = 0$ $0 + 64 = 64$ So the difference is $39 + 64 = 103°$

17. (a) 18   (b) 35   (c) 20 h^2 means h squared = h x h, etc.

18. A = 48°, B = 141°   Angles in a triangle add up to 180°, so A = 180 − 93 − 39 = 48°
Angles on a straight line add up to 180°, so B = 180 − 39 = 141°

19. 4 hours   Daily mean (average) = all the hours added together (28) ÷ the number of days (7)
28 ÷ 7 = 4 hours

20.

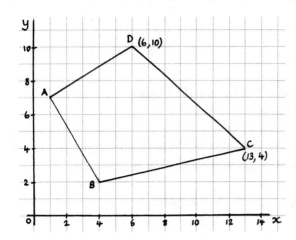

(a) kite ;   (b) right angle ;   (c) (5 , 6)

21. (i) 45   23 + 22 = 45 . The difference between the squares of two consecutive numbers
equals the sum of the original numbers.
(ii) 399   200 + 199 = 399
(iii) 2a − 1   a + (a − 1) = 2a − 1
(iv) 155   A negative (−) number multiplied by a negative number produces a positive (+)
number, so squares of all numbers, either positive or negative, are positive.

22. (a) 18   Altogether 55 things are ordered but there are only 37 tourists, so 55 − 37 = 18 order
both.

(b) 7   25 order a sandwich but 18 of them order both, so 25 − 18 = 7 order only sandwiches.

This can be shown by drawing a Venn diagram and fitting the numbers in.

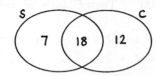

23. 11th   His birthday has two digits, so the possible day must be from 10 to 31. It is a prime number,
so it must be 11 or 13 or 17 or 19 or 23 or 29 or 31. The only one of these which is 2 more
than a square number is 11 which is 2 more than 9 (the square of 3).

24. (a) 8   Each of the 8 corner cubes has 3 painted faces.

     (b) 12   The middle cube on each edge of the large cube is painted on 2 faces.

     (c) 6   The central cube on each face of the large cube is painted on only 1 face.

     (d) 1   The small cube in the very centre of the large cube is not painted.

     (e) 8   The large cube has 8 cubes painted on 3 faces, 24 (= 2 x 12) cubes painted on 2 faces, 24 (= 4 x 6) cubes painted on only 1 face. Total of painted cubes 8 + 24 + 24 = 56.

                 Number of cubes in large square is 64, so number of unpainted cubes = 64 – 56 = 8. These are the 8 cubes in the centre of the large cube.

25. (a) 439, 440, 441   The mean of 1320 is 1320 ÷ 3 = 440. If 440 + 440 + 440 = 1320, then 439 + 440 + 441 = 1320.

     (b) 10, 11, 12   10 x 10 x 10 = 1000, so answer must be more than 10 x 10 x 10, etc.

26. (a) 8640   Volume = length x width x height = 30 x 24 x 12 = 8640 cm^3 (8640 cubic centimetres). Each 1 cm cube has volume 1 x 1 x 1 = 1 cm^3.

     (b) 216   6 bricks 5 cm long will fit into the total length of 30 cm

                 6 bricks 4 cm wide will fit into a total width of 24 cm, making a layer of 6 x 6 = 36 bricks

                 6 layers of bricks 2 cm high will fit into the total height of 12 cm, so the total number of bricks = 6 x 6 x 6 = 216

                 (Be careful! Sometimes in questions like this, the things inside boxes have to be fitted wrong way up, wrong way round, etc., to get the correct answer.)

27.

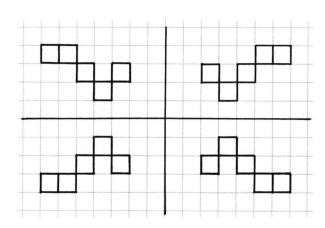

28. (i) 285 714 ; (ii) 428 571   7N + 1 = 1 000 000, so 7N = 999 999 and N = 142 857

     (iii) 571 428 , 714 285 , 857 142   Multiples of 142 857 up to 6x have the same digits in the same order, but starting at a different digit each time.

29. 90 seconds   They flash together again after the Lowest Common Multiple (LCM) of 18 and 15.

                 Prime factors of 18 = 2 x 3 x 3 ; prime factors of 15 = 3 x 5

                 LCM is highest number of 2s x highest number of 3s x highest number of 5s.

                 2 x 3 x 3 x 5 = 90

30. (a) 50p (or £0.50)   If Maddy had bought twice her amount (2 fruit pies + **6 buns**) she would have paid £2.40 x 2 = **£4.80**

                 Sarah bought 2 fruit pies + **2 buns**, and paid **£2.80**, so 4 buns cost £2.00

     (b) 90p (or £0.90)

PAPER B. Answers and explanations.

1. 4801

2. (a) 8   (b) 67

3. 4416

$$
\begin{array}{r}
1\,3\,8 \\
\times\ \ \ \ 3\,2 \\
\hline
2\,7\,6 \\
4\,1\,4\,\mathbf{0} \\
\hline
4\,4\,1\,6
\end{array}
$$

4. 317

5. A = 475, B = 650, C = 725   Each quarter of 100 (each small section) = 25

6. (a) $1\frac{1}{6}$ $1\frac{3}{4} = \frac{7}{4}$; $\frac{7}{4} \times \frac{2}{3}$ Divide top and bottom by 2. $\frac{7}{2} \times \frac{1}{3} = \frac{7}{6} = 1\frac{1}{6}$

    (b) $2\frac{5}{12}$ Lowest common denominator of 4 and 3 is 12

$$1 + \frac{9}{12} + \frac{8}{12} = 1 + \frac{17}{12} = 2\frac{5}{12}$$

7. 18·005   Columns are important. Write the decimal points first, in a straight column. Then write the numbers. Remember than 6 = 6·0

$$
\begin{array}{r}
1\,0\cdot4\,2 \\
1\cdot5\,8\,5 \\
+\ \ \ 6\cdot0 \\
\hline
1\,8\cdot0\,0\,5
\end{array}
$$

8. (a) 228 square inches   Areas of faces are {(9x6) + (9x4) + (6x4)} x 2 = (54 + 36 + 24) x 2 = 228
    (b) 216 cubic inches   9 x 6 x 4 = 216
    (c) 36 square inches   The cube root of 216 is 6.   6 x 6 x 6 = 216, so each edge of the cube is 6 inches long. 6 x 6 = 36

9. C   Area of B is 9x4=36, so each of the others has an area of 36. Perimeter of A is 6+6+6+6 = 24; perimeter of B is 9+4+9+4 = 26; perimeter of C is 12+3+12+3 = **30**; perimeter of D is 8+ $4\frac{1}{2}$ +8+ $4\frac{1}{2}$ = 25.

10. 40, 33   Subtracting 7 each time.
    25, $12\frac{1}{2}$ Dividing by 2 each time.

11. (a) $\frac{9}{20}$
    (b) 45%   To change a fraction into a percentage, multiply by 100 : $\frac{9}{20} \times \frac{100}{1} = 45\%$
    (c) 0·55   20 – 9 = 11.   11 divided by 20 = 0·55

12. (a) £6.60   (b) £1, 50p, 10p

13. (a) 19 $6\frac{1}{2} \times 4 = 26$;   26 – 6 = 20 ;   20 ÷ 2 = 10 ;   10 + 9 = 19
    (b) –2   2 – 9 = –7 ;   –7 x 2 = –14 ;   –14 + 6 = –8 ;   –8 ÷ 4 = –2

14. (a) 8   (b) 12   'All the way round' is 360° which represents 48 children.

MUSEUM: 60° which is $\frac{1}{6}$ of 360°, representing $\frac{1}{6}$ of 48 = 8.

PARK: Half the children = 24 which is is represented by 180°.

Park + Library + Museum = 180° + 30° + 60° = 270°, so 90° are left.

CINEMA: 90° which represents 12 children.

15. 93   Divide 372 by 4 = 93. Larger number is 93 x 3 = 279, smaller number is 93. 279 + 93 = 372

16. (a) (6 , 5)   (b) (2 , 6)   (c) (3½ , 3½)

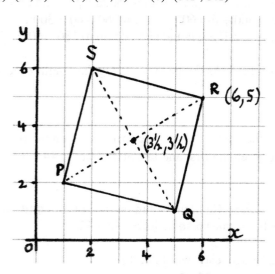

17. 70·00 , 7·000 , 0·770 , 0·707 , 0·070 , 0·007

Arrange like a decimal sum to show different sizes

0·070	(7 hundredths)
70·00	(7 tens)
0·770	(7 tenths and 7 hundredths)
0·007	(7 thousandths)
7·000	(7 units)
0·707	(7 tenths, 0 hundredths, 7 thousandths)

18. (a) acute   If K is obtuse (more than 90° but less than 180°) the other angles inside the triangle must both be acute.

(b) 103°   Angles on a straight line add up to 180°.   180 − 77 = 103°

(c) 22°   Angles in a triangle add up to 180°.   180 − 103 − 55 = 22°

19. £66   The charity has raised 89%, so they need another 100 − 89 = 11%

11% of £600 is £66.

20. (a) 4 $3w + 5 = 17$ $3w = 17 - 5 = 12$ $w = 12 \div 3 = 4$

(b) 7 $11w = 35 + 6w$ $11w - 6w = 35$ $5w = 35$ $w = 35 \div 5 = 7$

(c) 48 $\frac{2w}{3} = 32$ $2w = 32 \times 3 = 96$ $w = 96 \div 2 = 48$

21. (a) A   It takes 48 minutes.

(b) 42 minutes   Train C.

(c) 2   The 1544 and the 1738 from Idsley.

(d) 39 minutes   She must wait for the 1714 from Idsley. The 1644 does not stop at Keeton Green.

22. 1st January 2101   01/01/01

23. 15   4 years from now, Mark will be 9, so he is now 5. Mark is half William's age so William is 10. Philip is 7 years older than Mark so he is 12. Douglas is between Philip and William so he is 11. Four years from now, he will be 15.

24. (i) regular hexagon

    (ii) 300°   The hexagon is regular, so all its sides are equal. Angles round a point add up to 360° so the acute angle at the centre is $360 \div 6 = 60°$. $x = 360 - 60 = 300°$.

    (iii) 60°   The two angles in the triangle at A and B are equal and add up to $180 - 60 = 120°$, so angle $y = 120 \div 2 = 60°$

    (iv) 120°   The two angles at A are $60 + 60 = 120°$. As the hexagon is regular, angle z must also be 120°

25. 49 metres   The space between each tree and the next is 3·5 m. The space between the first 2 trees is **1** x 3·5, so the space between the first and last of **15** trees is **14** x 3·5 = 49 m

26. 15, 21, 25, 27, 35   Darren's number is 5, 7 or 9, so Charlene's number must be an **odd** multiple of one of these numbers but it must also be lower than 42.

27. (i) 13   If Amber and and Bella were both the same age, each would be 17.

            Sum of uncles' ages would be $(17 \times 2) + (17 \times 3) = $ **85** (Too many!).

        If Amber were 16 and Bella were 18, sum of uncles' ages would be $(16 \times 3) + (18 \times 2) = $ **84** (Still too many!). This gives a clue to the answer.

        (The answer can also be found by solving simultaneous equations.)

    (ii) 42

28. (a) 3, 4 and 5   The units answer is a 2 so L + M + N must equal 12. The only set of consecutive (one after another) digits which add up to 12 are 3, 4 and 5. $345 + 534 + 453 = 1332$.

    (b) 1, 2 and 3   Half of 1332 must have a 6 in the units column. The only set of consecutive digits smaller than 3, 4 and 5 to give this answer (666) is 1, 2 and 3.

    (c) 7, 8 and 9   Twice 1332 must have a 4 in the units column. The only set of consecutive digits bigger than 3, 4 and 5 to give this answer (2664) is 7, 8 and 9 which, when added, make 24.

29. The surround has a larger area by 1 cm^2.

                       The area of the card is $17 \times 17 = 289$. The area of the photograph is $12 \times 12 = $ **144** cm^2, so the area of the surround is $289 - 144 = $ **145** cm^2

30. (i) 55 cm $H = (7 \times 4) + (3 \times 9) = 28 + 27 = 55$

    (ii) 3 big boxes, 5 little boxes   3 big boxes height 21 cm + 5 little boxes height 15 cm = 36 cm

                                         This is the only mixture of boxes which gives a total height of 36 cm.

PAPER C. Answers and explanations.

1. 5353

2. 5353

3. 27

4. 259

5. (a) 3 , 48   Multiplying by 2 each time.

    (b) $10\frac{1}{2}$, $3\frac{1}{2}$, 0   Subtracting $3\frac{1}{2}$ each time.

6. 25·918   Line up decimal points first. Remember that 8 = 8·0

$$
\begin{array}{r}
0\cdot868 \\
8\cdot0 \\
+\ \ 17\cdot05 \\
\hline
25\cdot918
\end{array}
$$

7. 30 $3\frac{3}{4} = \frac{15}{4} = \frac{30}{8}$

8. (a) 15·8
    (b) 18·4
    (c) 17·1   Add the two numbers and divide the result by 2.

9. h = 44°   Alternate angles (in a Z shape between parallel lines) are equal.
    j = 133°   The angle to the left of j is 47° (alternate). Angles on a straight line = 180°.
                    j = 180 − 47 = 133°
    k = 89°   Angles on a straight line = 180°.   180° − 47° − 44° = 89°

10. (a) 30 000 000
    (b) fifteen thousand and fifty

11. 25m   Rayyan has run 150 ÷ 2 = 75m; Lewis has run 150 ÷ 3 = 50m.

12. (i) 23   2j + 5h = 8 + 15 = 23
    (ii) −16   h + 3k − 4j = 3 − 3 − 16 = −16   (+ − 3 means −3)
    (iii) 48 j^2 × h = 4 × 4 × 3 = 48   (j^2 = j × j)

13. (i) 80 cm   Area of rectangle = length × width. If b = 4, a = 144 ÷ 4 = 36. Perimeter is
                    36+4+36+4 = 80
    (ii) 60 cm   If b = 6, a = 144 ÷ 6 = 24. Perimeter is 24+6+24+6 = 60
    (iii) 52 cm   If b = 8, a = 144 ÷ 8 = 18. Perimeter is 18+8+18+8 = 52
    (iv) 12   The shortest perimeter happens when the rectangle becomes a square.
                  Square root of 144 is 12, so perimeter is 12+12+12+12 = 48 which is the shortest
                   possible perimeter.

14. (a) £1.77
    (b) 5   Coins are £1, 50p, 20p, 5p and 2p.

    (c) 18   She needs £10.00 − £6.40 = £3.60 or 360p.   360 ÷ 20 = 18

15. 19   Morning Herald angle is 360 − 125 − 80 − 60 = 95°. $\frac{95}{360}$ × 72 = 19

16. 13:45 (*or* 1345 *or* 13 45)　　　　Journey takes 3 h 35 min + 15 min = 3 h 50.　09:55 + 03 50 = 13:45

17. (a) 7 June　　　　Ten days from 28 May is 29, 30, 31, 1 June, 2, 3, 4, 5, 6, **7**

　　(b) Friday　　　　Counting backwards from 7 June　7　6　5　4　3　2　1　31　30　29　28
　　　　　　　　　　　　　　　　　　　　　　　　　　M　Su　Sa　F　Th　W　Tu　M　Su　Sa　**F**

18.

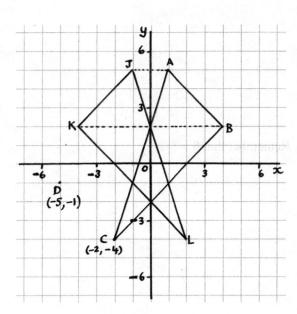

　　(c) isosceles trapezium
　　(d) (−5 , −1)

19. 120g　　　　Toffees to fill half the tin weigh　470 − 295 = 175g
　　　　　　　　　Toffees to fill the whole tin weigh　175 × 2 = 350g
　　　　　　　　　Tin weighs 470 − 350 = 120g

20. (a) £6
　　(b) £126
　　(c) £132.30　　　　　　5% of £126 = £6.30　　　　£126 + £6.30 = £132.30

21. (a) 28　　　　Number of squares increases by 1 more each time
　　　　　　　　　Term　　1　　2　　3　　4　　5　　6　　7
　　　　　　　　　Squares　1　　3　　6　　10　　15　　21　　**28**
　　　　　　　　　Increase　+2　+3　+4　+5　+6　+7

　　(b) 44　　　　Number of stars increases by 1 more each time
　　　　　　　　　Term　　1　　2　　3　　4　　5　　6　　7　　8
　　　　　　　　　Stars　　2　　5　　9　　14　　20　　27　　35　　**44**
　　　　　　　　　Increase　+3　+4　+5　+6　+7　+8　+9

22. 36　　　　Find the difference between the opposite numbers. Then multiply by 2.
　　　　　　　　　23 − 5 = 18.　　18 × 2 = 36
　　　　　　　　(This can be most easily seen on a clock face, e.g. 2 is directly opposite 8.
　　　　　　　　　8 − 2 = 6.　　6 × 2 = 12)

23. (a) 6　　　　61 − 13 = 48　　　　48 ÷ 8 = 6
　　(b) 9　　　　Single-digit numbers whose squares have 2 digits are　4, 5, 6, 7, 8 and 9
　　　　　　　　　$9^2 = 81$　　　Digits of 81 are 8 and 1 which add up to 9.

24. 2.45 p.m.

Train A: 7.15 a.m. , 8.45 , 10.15 , 11.45 , 1.15 p.m. , **2.45 p.m.**
Train B: 7.15 a.m. , 9.45 , 12.15 p.m. , **2.45 p.m.**
or Lowest Common Multiple (L.C.M.) of $1\frac{1}{2}$ hours and $2\frac{1}{2}$ hours is $7\frac{1}{2}$ hours, so trains both leave the station together again at 07 15 + 7 30 = 14 45 or 2.45 p.m.

25. £26

Total money is £37 + £89 = £126.   £126 ÷ 2 = £63 each.
Leon £37 + £26 = £63; Abigail £89 – £26 = £63

26.

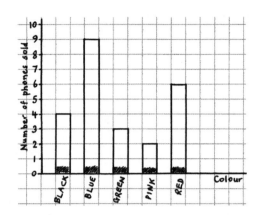

27. (a) $\frac{2}{5}$

25 gums altogether. Purple gums $\frac{10}{25} = \frac{2}{5}$

(b) $\frac{5}{8}$

There are now 15 orange and 9 purple. 24 gums altogther. $\frac{15}{24} = \frac{5}{8}$

28. 9

Volume of tank = 40 x 20 x 30 = 24 000 cm³ = 24 litres
$\frac{3}{4}$ of 24 = 18, so 9 jugfuls are needed

29. (a) 235 m

Real length of pond = 94 x 2 500 = 235 000 mm = 235 m

(b) 120 mm

Length of road on map = 300 000 mm ÷ 2 500 = 120 mm

30. 6·25% or $6\frac{1}{4}$%

After 6 hours, radioactivity is half of 100 = 50% of original.
After 12 hours, it is half of 50 = 25%.
After 18 hours it is half of 25 = 12·5%.
After 24 hours it is half of 12·5 = 6·25%.

PAPER D. Answers and explanations.

1. 5051

2. 1338

3. Thirty three thousand and sixty six

4. 527 $3689 \div 7 = 527$

5. $13\frac{1}{2}$ or 13·5

6. (a) 7, 11, 15   Adding 4 each time.
   (b) 120, 60, 30   Dividing by 2 each time.

7. 0·3   3·0 is the largest, then 0·33, then <u>0·3</u>

8. (i) A $\frac{1}{2}$; B $\frac{3}{8}$; C $\frac{1}{4}$

    (ii) $1\frac{1}{8}$ Convert all to eighths, as 8 is the lowest common denominator
                  $\frac{4}{8} + \frac{3}{8} + \frac{2}{8} = \frac{9}{8} = 1\frac{1}{8}$

9. 480 ml   12 litres = 12 000 millilitres. $12\,000 \div 25 = 480$

10. £1.61

11. (i) −2
    (ii) 20
    (iii) 48
    (iv) 3 $5 + 4 = 9$. The square root of 9 is 3

12. (a) 47 m² (b) 46 m

13. b = 33°   In bottom $\triangle$, top left angle is 57° (opposite angles in an X shape). a is 90°.
                  Angles in $\triangle$ add up to 180°. $180 - 57 - 90 = 33$
    c = 29°   In top $\triangle$, bottom left angle is 123° (angles on a straight line add up to 180°)
                  Bottom right angle is 28° (angles on a straight line). $180 - 123 - 28 = 29$

14. (a) 7   Reverse the process from the result: $8 \times 2 = 16$; $16 + 5 = 21$; $21 \div 3 = 7$

    (b) $\frac{1}{2}$ Same again: $-1\frac{3}{4} \times 2 = -3\frac{1}{2}$; $-3\frac{1}{2} + 5 = 1\frac{1}{2}$; $1\frac{1}{2} \div 3 = \frac{1}{2}$

15. 52   Angle for lorries is $360 - 243 - 39 = 78°$. $\frac{78}{360} \times 240 = 52$

16. 3   If none is to be left over, the least number of biscuits she can buy is the lowest common
         multiple of 8 and 12 which is 24. This means buying 2 packets of Rocky and 3 packets of
         Crummy.

17.

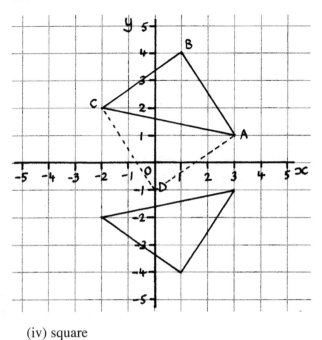

(iv) square

18. 9

	×	
	11	15
12		

	×	10
	11	15
12		

	×	10
	11	15
12		8

14	×	10
	11	15
12		8

14	9	10
	11	15
12		8

19. (a) 45   45 occurs more times than any other number so it is the mode.

(b) 44   Numbers in order of size are   37, 41, 42, **44**, 45, 45, 47
            44 is the middle number (the median).

(c) 43   Mean is total amount divided by number of things. $301 \div 7 = 43$

(d) 10   Lowest number is 37; highest is 47. Range is $47 - 37 = 10$

20. (a) 2368   (b) 8623   (c) 6300

21. (i) A and C
(ii) B, C and D

22. (a) 4462

$$\begin{array}{r} 97 \\ \times 46 \\ \hline 582 \\ 3880 \\ \hline 4462 \end{array}$$

(b) 0·4462   4 decimal places in question, so 4 places in answer

(c) 2231   97 × 23 is half of 97 × 46

(d) 2254   23 more than 2231

23. 285 g   Left-hand balance.   Left side 5 x 95 = 475 g;   right side   2B + 95 = 475 g
              Block of material B weighs 190 g.
           Right-hand balance.   Right side (5 x 95) + (2 x 190) = 855g ; left side   570 + C = 855 g.
              Block of material C weighs 285 g.

24. (a) £594   8% of £550 is £44.   £500 + £44 = £594
     (b) £712.80   20% of £594 is £118.80.   £594 + £118.80 = £712.80

25. 24   Starting with bell A, there are 6 different orders: ABCG, ABGC, ACBG, ACGB, AGBC, AGCB.
         Starting with bell B there are 6 more, with bell C another 6 and with bell D another 6.
            (**or**   4 x 3 x 2 x 1 = 24)

26. (a)

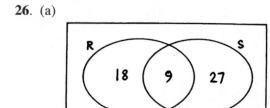

     (b) 64   18 + 9 + 27 + 10 = 64

27. 05:03   9 hours later than 19:43 is (28:43 – 24 hours as it the next day) 04:43 + 20 min = 05:03

28. 24   95 + 47 = 142.   142 ÷ 2 = 71.   24 bricks must be moved from the smaller pile to make the
         piles equal.

29. 13 000 cm³   Volume of block = 50 x 30 x 10 = 15 000 cm³.

            Area of triangle = $\frac{\text{base x height}}{2}$, so the volume of the hole is 10 x 20 x 10 = 2 000 cm³

            15 000 – 2 000 = 13 000

30. Length 12m; width 8m.   If you know how to do simultaneous equations, the working is easy, but if
                      not:-
     Perimeter of a rectangle is 2(L + W) = 2L + 2W.
     Supposing the Jones family had enlarged the garden to be twice the width **and twice the length** of
       the original. The perimeter of the new garden would have been 2(2L + 2W) = **4L + 4W = 80m**.
     As the length is actually **3 times** the original, the perimeter is 2(3L + 2W) = **6L + 4W = 104 m**.
     From these two results, 2L = 24, so L = 12, and from there, going back to the original garden, W = 8.

PAPER E. Answers and explanations.

1. 808

2. 737

3. 5445

4. 42   7 squared is 49.   49 – 7 = 42

5. (a) $\frac{3}{4}$ (b) 25

6. 10·89   Line up decimal points first. Remember that 4 = 4·0

$$\begin{array}{r} 6 \cdot 3\,2 \\ 0 \cdot 5 \\ 4 \cdot 0 \\ +\quad 0 \cdot 0\,7 \\ \hline 1\,0 \cdot 8\,9 \end{array}$$

7. 1 043 092

8. (a) 3 087   (b) 3 087   (c) 3 087

9. (i) A 12·10 ; B 12·70 ; C 13·15   Each small division represents 0·05

   (ii) 0·45   Difference means subtract smaller number from larger number.

10. (a) 16, 8   Dividing by 2 each time.
   (b) 35, 38   Adding 3 and 4 alternately

11. 115°   Bottom angle of Δ is 81° (opposite angles in an X shape are equal). Angle at top right of Δ is 34° (angles on a straight line add up to 180°). Angle at top left of Δ is 65° (angles in a triangle add up to 180°), so x = 180 – 65 = 115°.

12. (a) 6 h 25 min   From 8.50 to 12.00 mid-day is 3 h 10 min. From 12.00 to 3.15 is 3 h 15 min.   3 h 10 min + 3 h 15 min = 6 h 25 min

   (b) Start 08:50 ; end 15:15 (*or* 0850 and 1515, *or* 08 50 and 15 15)

13. (a) $\frac{2}{3}$ $\frac{24}{36}$ are not black. This simplifies to $\frac{2}{3}$.

   (b)

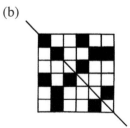

14. (a) 6·5°C   A 'thermometer line' may be helpful.

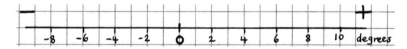

   (b) 2°C   Rise in temperature was 18°; number of hours was 9.   18° ÷ 9 = 2°

15. £3.90 $\frac{3}{5}$ of £9.50 = £5.70.   2 adults at £9.50 and 3 children at £5.70 makes £36.10

16. 30%   Angle for COAL = 360 − 54 − 162 − 36 = 108°. $\frac{108}{360} = \frac{3}{10} = 30\%$

17. (a) 4 200 mm   Car length is 14 × 12 = 168 inches.   168 × 25 = 4 200
     (b) 6 feet   Car width is 1800 ÷ 25 = 72 inches.   72 ÷ 12 = 6

18. Addition   4 7 **3**   Units column: answer must be 12, so missing digit is 3
                6 8   Tens column: 1 + 7 + 6 + ? = 16 , so missing digit is 2
      +   9 **2** 1   Answer: 1 + 9 + 4 = 14, so missing digit is 4
          —————
        1 **4** 6 2

Division   9 **7**   5 x 9 = 45, so missing digit in bottom line is 4.
          —————
      5) **4** 8 5   48 ÷ 5 = 9 remainder 3.   35 ÷ 5 = 7, so missing digit in top line is 7.

19. (a) 324   (b) 125   (c) 12   (d) −3

20. (i) t = 7
     (ii) w = 24

21.

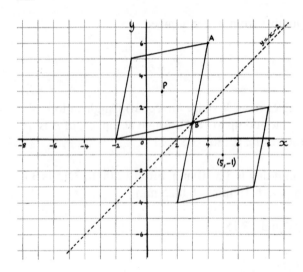

(An easy way to draw the rhombus is to draw diagonals first, then join up the corners.)

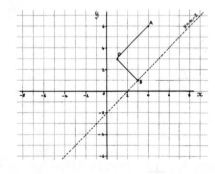

(ii) (−2 , 0), (−1 , 5)
(iv) (5 , −1)

16 − **E**

22. Green bus by 8 minutes   Red bus goes 20 miles. At 15 miles/hour it takes $1\frac{1}{3}$ hour = 1 h 20 min

Green bus goes 24 miles. At 20 miles/hour it takes $1\frac{1}{5}$ hour = 1 h 12 min

23. F = $8\frac{1}{2}$; G = 1 ; H = 9   Multiply by 2; then add 5

24. 6 m

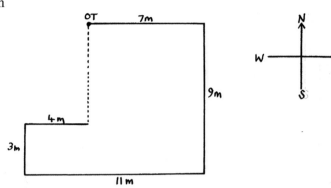

25. (a) 2011   Year cannot be 2004, 2006, 2008, 2010, 2012, 2014 or 2016 as they divide by 2.
It cannot be 2007 or 2013 as they divide by 3. It cannot be 2005 or 2015 as they
divide by 5. It cannot be 2009 as it divides by 7. The only remaining year is 2011
(2011 is a prime number).

  (b) June

  (c) 29th   June has 30 days, so highest prime is 29

26. 22 miles   If she walked n miles on the first day, she walked n+3 on the second, n+6 on the
third day, n+9 on the fourth day and n+12 on the fifth day.
n + (n+3) + (n+6) + (n+9) + (n+12) = 5n + 30 = 125, so n = 95 ÷ 5 = 19
She walked 19 miles on the first day, and 19 + 3 = 22 miles on the second day.

27. 490 m³   End wall: area of rectangle = 7 x 3·5 = 24·5 m²

area of triangle = $\frac{\text{base x height}}{2}$ = $\frac{7 \times 3}{2}$ = 10·5 m²

Total area of end wall = 24·5 + 10·5 = 35 m². Inside space = 35 x 14 = 490 m³

28. 55 mm   2.2 m = 2200 mm. 2200 ÷ 40 = 55

29. (a) 1 618   100 + 500 + 100 + 10 + 5 + 1 + 1 + 1

  (b) MMCCCLXXI   2000 = MM; 300 = CCC; 50 = L; 20 = XX; I = 1

30. 381 cm³   7 steps.   3 + 6 + 12 + 24 + 48 + 96 + 192 = 381

PAPER F. Answers and explanations.

1. 3 325

2. 43 806

3.   2772
+ 5885
  8657

4. 1 523

5. 2, 3, 5, 7, 11, 13, 17, 19, 23, 29

6. (i) 58 ;   (ii) 40 ;   (iii) $8\frac{1}{2}$

7. (a) $\frac{2}{5}$ $\frac{6}{15} = \frac{2}{5}$

(b) 0·4
(c) 60%

8. (a) $1\frac{7}{12}$ Whole numbers: $2 - 1 = 1$. Fractions: Lowest common denominator of 6 and 4 is 12.
$\frac{5}{6} - \frac{1}{4} = \frac{10}{12} - \frac{3}{12} = \frac{7}{12}$

(b) $4\frac{1}{2}$ Change to improper (top-heavy) fractions if needed. $\frac{16}{5} \times \frac{3}{4} \times \frac{15}{8} = \frac{9}{2} = 4\frac{1}{2}$

(c) $\frac{2}{3}$ $\frac{5}{8} \div \frac{15}{16} = \frac{5}{8} \times \frac{16}{15} = \frac{2}{3}$

9. 19 cm   7 days in a week ; $218 - 85 = 133$; $133 \div 7 = 19$

10. £152.25

11. (a) parallelogram
(b) trapezium
(c) 38°   ABCDE is isosceles, so obtuse angle at E equals obtuse angle at C = 109°
Angles on a straight line = 180°, so acute angle at E is 180 – 109 = 71°
Δ ADE is isosceles so angle in Δ ADE at D also equals 71°
x = 180 – 71 – 71 = 38°

12. 58 cm   Area of rectangle is 8 times area of shaded triangle $8 \times 26 = 208$ cm²
Longer side of rectangle is 16 cm, so shorter side is 208 ÷ 16 = 13 cm
16 + 13 + 16 + 13 = 58

13. (a) 31, 25, 19   Subtracting 6 each time
(b) 1, 3, 9   Multiplying by 3 each time

14. 270   Length of floor is 5·4 m = 540 cm. Number of tiles is 540 ÷ 30 = 18
Width of floor is 4·5 m = 450 cm. Number of tiles is 450 ÷ 30 = 15
15 x 18 = 270

15. (i) 19   (ii) $4\frac{1}{2}$ or 4·5   (iii) 23   5ab means 5 x a x b = 5 x 3 x 2 = 30

16.

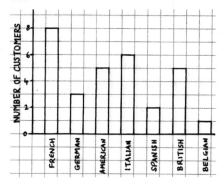

17. (a) 60°   (or 300°)

(b) 15°   (or 345°)

(c) 130°   (or 230°)

Each hour, the hour (small) hand moves through 360 ÷ 12 = 30°

At half past six, hour hand is half way between 6 and 7, which is 15°

At twenty past eight, minute hand points to 4; hour hand is one third of the way between 8 and 9, which is 10°

18. (a) 3 h 40 min

From 10.00 a.m. (10:00) to 1.40 p.m. (13:40)   is 13:40 − 10:00 = 3 h 40 min

(b) 14 h 50 min

Train sets off again 4 h 40 min after 1.40 p.m. which is 6.20 p.m.

From 6.20 p.m. to 6.20 a.m. on Thursday it takes 12 hours.

From 6.20 a.m. to 9.10 a.m. on Thursday it takes 2 h 50 min, so altogether the journey takes 12 hours + 2 h 50 min = 14h 50 min.

19.

(i)

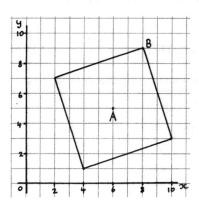

(ii) 40 square units

The area of the large square is 8 × 8 = 64 square units.

Each of the 4 'extra' triangles at the corners has an area of $\frac{1}{2}$ × base × height = 6.

Total area of triangles is 6 × 4 = 24, so area of original square is 64 − 24 = 40 square units.

(*or* without calculating area of large square)

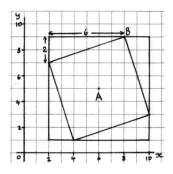 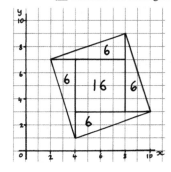

20. [a] 11 ; [b] 17 ; [c] 0 ; [d] 33 Work out brackets first (e.g. in question [b] the bracket is 7 − 1 = 6). Then do multiplication and division (if any), then addition and subtraction (if any).

21. 408 First shell has 8 small squares; second shell has 2 × 8 = 16 squares; third shell has 3 × 8 = 24 squares, etc., so the fifty-first shell has 51 × 8 = 408 squares.

22. (a) 720 $6! = 6 \times 5 \times 4 \times 3 \times 2 \times 1 = 720$

(b) 5040 $7! = 7 \times 6! = 7 \times 720 = 5040$

(c) 7 $5040 \div 720 = 7$

(d) 20 Just as **7**! ÷ 6! = **7**, so **8**! ÷ 7! = **8**, etc.

23. (a) 40% $100 - 25 - 35 = 40$

(b) 160 40% of flock = 64 sheep, so 10% = 64 ÷ 4 = 16 sheep, so 100% = 160 sheep.

24. 120 kg Rob weighs $\frac{1}{2}$ of 90 kg = 45 kg ; Lara weighs $\frac{1}{3}$ of 90 kg = 30 kg;

Freddie weighs $\frac{1}{5}$ of 90 kg = 18 kg ; Kate weighs $\frac{3}{10}$ of 90 kg = 27 kg.

25. (a) $\frac{2}{5}$ There are 10 balls altogether. 4 are yellow. Probability is $\frac{4}{10} = \frac{2}{5}$

(b) $\frac{1}{3}$ There are now only 9 balls. 3 are yellow. Probability is $\frac{3}{9} = \frac{1}{3}$

26. 1320 litres The tank was $\frac{1}{4}$ full and is now $\frac{7}{8}$ full, so Duncan has added $\frac{7}{8} - \frac{1}{4} = \frac{5}{8}$.

$\frac{5}{8}$ of the tank = 825, so the tank holds $\frac{825}{5} \times 8 = 1320$ litres.

27. (a) 17 20 wore neither, so 68 − 20 = 48 wore either a hat or glasses or both.
36 + 29 = 65 wore either or both, but there were only 48 people, so 65 − 48 = 17 wore both.

(b) 12 29 wore a hat, but 17 of these also wore glasses. That leaves 29 − 17 = 12.

This can be shown by drawing a Venn diagram and fitting the numbers in.

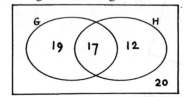

28. (a) 9

(b) 170 Number of diagonals in a 20-sided figure is $\frac{20(20-3)}{2} = \frac{20 \times 17}{2} = \frac{340}{2} = 170$

(c) 10 $\frac{x(x-3)}{2} = 35$; $x^2 - 3x = 70$; $100 - 30 = 70$

29. 14 10 layers would be 75 × 10 = 750 mm high. Another 3 layers (13 layers) would be 975 mm high, but this would not quite be 1 metre, so 14 layers would be needed.

30. 4567 The number is prime, so it cannot be 1234 or 3456 or 5678 because they divide by 2.
It cannot be 0123 or 6789 because they divide by 3.
It cannot be 2345 because it divides by 5.
4567 is the only four-digit consecutive combination which is also a prime number.
(None of the reverse consecutives is prime either, e.g. 9876, 6543, 3210, etc.)

PAPER G. Answers and explanations.

1. 3333

2. 888

3. 3456

4. 444

5. 60 070

6. P 11·50 , Q 12·75 , R 13·25 Each square is one quarter (or 0·25)

7. (a) x , + (b) ÷ , –

8. (a) $\frac{2}{5}$ (b) $\frac{5}{12}$ 12 is lowest common denominator : $\frac{6+8-9}{12} = \frac{5}{12}$

9. £4 500

10. 100·899

$$\begin{array}{r} 0\cdot009 \\ 9\cdot \\ 0\cdot9 \\ +\quad 0\cdot99 \\ 90\cdot \\ \hline 100\cdot899 \end{array}$$

11. (a) 36 cm
(b) 27 cm^2 Area of rectangle is 12 x 6 = 72 cm^2. Area of bottom left-hand triangle is 36 cm^2.
Area of top right-hand Δ is $\frac{6 \times 3}{2}$ = 9 cm^2. Area of shaded part is 36 – 9 = 27 cm^2.

12. 0·88 , $\frac{7}{8}$, 86% , $\frac{6}{7}$, 0·8 Change fractions and percentages to decimals. Then compare sizes.

13. 77° All the way round is 360°. 360 – 52 = 308 ; 308 ÷ 4 = 77°

14. (a) 8 cm^3 4 x 2 x 1 = 8
(b) 216 cm^3 12 x 6 x 3 = 216
(c) 1 : 27 216 ÷ 8 = 27

15. 53p or £0.53 Total purchases £5.47 ; 6.00 – 5.47 = 0.53

16.

6	7	2
1	5	9
8	3	4

		2
1	5	

		2
1	5	
8		

6		2
1	5	
8		

6	7	2
1	5	
8		4

6	7	2
1	5	9
8	3	4

17. (i) 2d ; (ii) 0 ; (iii) d² ; (iv) 1 ; (v) $15\frac{1}{2}$

(vi) 9   A negative multiplied by a negative (– × –) gives a positive (+) result.

18.

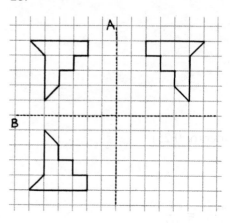

19. 1089

20. w = 29°   Corresponding angles (angles in same position on parallel lines) are equal.
     x = 48°   Angle at bottom left of Δ is 48° (angles on a straight line add up to 180°). So x must
                  be the same size (corresponding angles again).
     y = 103°   Bottom two angles in Δ add up to 77°.   180 – 77 = 103° (angles in a Δ = 180°)

21. 1.05 p.m.   From 8.40 a.m. to 4.40 p.m. is 8 hours, so from 8.40 a.m. to 5.30 p.m. is 8 h 50 min.
                 Half of 8h 50 min is 4h 25 min.   4 h 25 min after 8.40 a.m. is 1.05 p.m.

22. (a) 64 $2^3 = 2 \times 2 \times 2 = 8.$ $8^2 = 64$

(b) $\frac{9}{16}$

(c) 1 $(-1)^2 = -1 \times -1 = +1.$ $1^3 = 1 \times 1 \times 1 = 1$

23. (a) 175 m $35 \times 5\,000 = 175\,000$ mm = 175 m
     (b) 52 mm   260 m = 260 000 mm.   260 000 mm ÷ 5 000 = 52 mm

24.

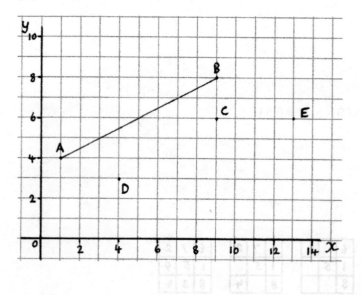

24. (continued)

Gradient of AC is 25% $\frac{2}{8} = \frac{1}{4} = 25\%$

Gradient of DE is 33% $\frac{3}{9} = \frac{1}{3} = 33\%$ to nearest whole number.   (Accurately 33·3 recurring.)

Gradient of AE is 17% $\frac{2}{12} = \frac{1}{6} = 17\%$ to nearest whole number.   (Accurately 16·6 recurring.)

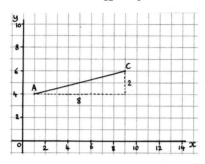
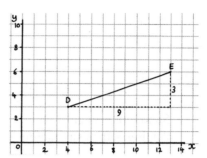

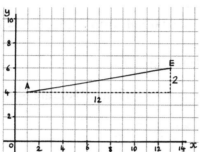

25. 36 days   Lowest common multiple (L.C.M.) of 4, 6 and 9 is 36

26. 17   If Kieran's age is K, Myles's age is K – 3 and Ronan's age is K + 5.
                              K + (K – 3) + (K + 5) = 53, so 3K + 2 = 53.   3K = 51.   K = 17

27. (a) 16:00   30 ÷ 15 = 2 ; **East** of London, so 2 hours **later** than London.

  (b) 07:00   105 ÷ 15 = 7 ; **West** of London, so 7 hours **earlier** than London.

  (c) 01:00 (the next day)   165 ÷ 15 = 11 ; **East** of London, so 11 hours **later** than London.

  (d) 90   05:30 is 6 hours earlier than London ; 6 x 15° = 90°W

28. (a) 9   Add scores and divide by number of matches 54 ÷ 6 = 9
     (b) 16   To reach an average (mean) of 10 in 7 matches, he needs 70 runs. 70 – 54 = 16

29. (a) 8 anticlockwise   B will rotate fewer times than A in the ratio $\frac{20}{30} = \frac{2}{3}$. $\frac{2}{3}$ x 12 = 8

  (b) 6 clockwise   C will rotate fewer times than B in the ratio $\frac{30}{40} = \frac{3}{4}$. $\frac{3}{4}$ x 8 = 6

30. 16 gallons   Gregg's car will need 2 520 ÷ 63 = 40 gallons (7 x 9 = 63, so it is easier to
                              divide by 7 and then by 9 to get the result).
                              Nev's car will need 2 520 ÷ 45 = 56 gallons (5 x 9 = 45, so it is easier to
                              divide by 5 and then by 9 to get the result).

PAPER H. Answers and explanations.

1. A = 95 ;   B = 69 ;   C = 3·5 or $3\frac{1}{2}$

2. 318

3. (a) 18 ;   (b) 9 ;   (c) 23

4. 7722

5. £64.50

6. (a) 900, 867   Subtracting 33 each time.
    (b) 13, 16   Adding 3, then subtracting 1.

7. 4 500   There are 75 minutes between 9.00 and 10.15.   75 × 60 = 4 500

8. A 48cm   Each square has a length of $\sqrt{9}$ = 3

    B 104cm²   Area of each square is 4 × 4 = 16cm². There are $6\frac{1}{2}$ squares. 16 × $6\frac{1}{2}$ = 104

9. (a) 8 $\frac{6}{1} \div \frac{3}{4}$ = $\frac{6}{1} \times \frac{4}{3}$ = $\frac{8}{1}$ = 8

    (b) $3\frac{3}{4}$ $\frac{1}{2} \times \frac{5}{6} \times \frac{9}{1}$ = $\frac{15}{4}$ = $3\frac{3}{4}$

    (c) 1 $\frac{5}{6} + \frac{1}{2} - \frac{1}{3}$ = $\frac{5}{6} + \frac{3}{6} - \frac{2}{6}$ = $\frac{6}{6}$ = 1

10. (a) 87   87 × 1p coins
    (b) 5   50p, 20p, 10p, 5p, 2p

11. (a) 30 ;   (b) −5 ;   (c) $\frac{3}{8}$

    (d) 7   d + e + de = 4 + 9 + 36 = 49. Square root of 49 is 7.

12. (a) $\frac{2}{5}$ Coloured rectangle: 7 whole squares + 10 half squares = 12 squares.
            Large rectangle 6 × 5 = 30 squares. $\frac{12}{30}$ = $\frac{2}{5}$

    (b) 8   One third of 30 = 10. To leave 10 squares uncoloured, 20 must be coloured.
            20 − 12 = 8

13. (a) 35p   3 people, so divide total money 114p by 3 to get equal shares. This is 38p.
            For Tammy to have 38p, she would have to give 73 − 38 = 35p

    (b) 20p   Ruth had 18p. After sharing she would have 38p, so her amount would have
            increased by 20p.

14. (a) 113°   Angles on a straight line add up to 180°.   180 − 67 = 113
    (b) 84°   Bottom right-hand angle in Δ is 29° (angles on a straight line).
            Angles in a Δ add up to 180°.   180 − 67 − 29 = 84

15. £11 050

Each Economy ticket costs £6 800 ÷ 8 = £850.
First Class ticket costs 3 times Economy ticket, which is 3 × £850 = £2 550.
Business Class ticket costs twice Economy ticket, which is 2 × 850 = £1 700.
(3 × 2 550) + (2 × 1 700) = 7 650 + 3 400 = 11 050

16. (a) 5·247

$2·7 + 1·35 + 0·9 + 0·27 + 0·027 = 5·247$

(b) 5 247

17. (a) 75°

$360 - 120 - 60 - 105 = 75$

(b)

5 ASH trees need 75°, so each tree needs 15°. There are 120 ÷ 15 = 8 OAK trees, etc.

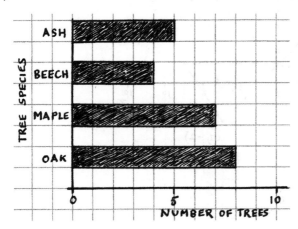

18. (a) £15.40

$22 \times \frac{70}{100} = \frac{154}{10} = 15.4$

(b) £30.00

$21 \times \frac{100}{70} = \frac{30}{1} = 30$ (*or* 10% is 21 ÷ 7 = 3, so 100% is 3 × 10 = 30).

19. (a) 5 vertices, 8 edges
(b) 6 faces, 12 edges
(c) 30

$20 + 12 = \mathbf{30} + 2$

20. 13

The squares of the numbers are 64 and 25.   64 − 25 = 39
The square roots of 64 and 25 are 8 and 5.   8 + 5 = 13

21. 10·8

Volume of bucket = area of base × height = 450 × 24 = 10800 cm^3
1 000 cm^3 (or 1 000 ml) = 1 litre.   10 800 ÷ 1 000 = 10·8

22.
  4327
− 1563
  2764

Units column: another possibility could be 17 − 8 = 9 but this does not work out in
   the other columns.
Tens column: another possibility could be 2 − 1 = 1 but this does not work out in the
   other columns.

23. x = 108°
   y = 48°

Angles on a straight line add up to 180°.   180 − 72 = 108
Each of the 3 angles in equilateral Δ CDF is 60° (angles in Δ add up to 180°).
Like angle x, each of the other **interior** angles in the pentagon is 108°.
y = 108 − 60 = 48°

24. (a) 373°K ;   (b) 310°K ;   (c) −27°C

25. 4

Lowest common multiple of 8, 12 and 6 is 24, so I buy the things every 24 days.
Number of loaves needed = 24 ÷ 6 = 4

26. 6   Multiplying each number by 2 does not give answers with identical digits.

Multiplying the first two numbers by 3 gives 141 × 3 = **423** and 108 × 3 = **324**. The possible answer could be 3, but the sum of the answers 423 + 324 + 243 + 432 + 234 + 342 is only 1998. This is half of 3996, so the required number is 3 × 2 = 6

27.

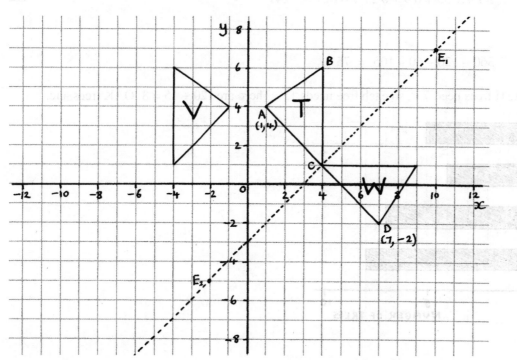

Coordinates of E are either (10 , 7) or (−2 , −5)

28. (a) $\frac{4}{9}$ If 20 are green, 16 are red.   16 out of 36 = 4 out of 9

     (b) $\frac{3}{7}$ Now there are only 35 apples. 15 out of 35 = 3 out of 7

29. (i) A: 8.42 ;   B: 9.11 ;   C: 9.16
     (ii) 28 minutes
     (iii) 11.50 a.m.
     (iv) 17 miles/h   The bus goes $4\frac{1}{4}$ miles in 15 minutes. At the same speed, in 1 hour (=60 minutes) it would go $4\frac{1}{4} \times 4 = 17$ miles

30. 22 square units   This is fairly easy if you know that the area of a rhombus with diagonals lengths **a** and **b** is $\frac{ab}{2}$.

If not, look at the top half of the inside rhombus. This is a triangle with base 8 units and height 6 units, so its area is (8 × 6) ÷ 2 = 24 square units, and the area of the complete rhombus is 24 × 2 = 48 square units.

Now look at the top half of the outside rhombus. This is a triangle with base 10 units and height 7 units, so its area is (10 × 7) ÷ 2 = 35 square units, and the area of the complete rhombus is 35 × 2 = 70 square units.

The area of the space between the two rhombuses is 70 − 48 = 22 square units

PAPER J. Answers and explanations.

1. 3434

2. 4343

3. 3344

4. 434

5. 13, 31   Adding one more each time: 4 **+2** 6 **+3** 9 **+4**, etc.
    1, –7   Subtracting 4 each time.

6. (a) 7.33 p.m.   1 hour before 9.11 was 8.11.   30 minutes (half an hour) before that was 7.41.
                       8 minutes before that was 7.33.   Total 1h 38 min

    (b) 21:11 (*or* 2111 *or* 21 11)

7. $\frac{2}{5}$, $\frac{3}{7}$, $\frac{4}{9}$, $\frac{9}{20}$ Change to decimals by dividing numerators (tops) by denominators (bottoms).
                      $4 \div 9 = 0\cdot\underline{444}.......$; $2 \div 5 = 0\cdot4$; $9 \div 20 = 0\cdot\underline{45}$; $3 \div 7 = 0\cdot\underline{428}.......$

8. 114°   AB = AC (isosceles Δ) so angles inside triangle at B and C are each 66° (angles in a
            Δ add up to 180°); $180 - 48 = 132$; $132 \div 2 = 66$
            $x = 180° - 66° = 114°$ (angles on a straight line add up to 180°)

9. 7   Eva has $\frac{1}{5}$ of 40 = 8, Mia has $\frac{1}{4}$ of 40 = 10, Annabel has $\frac{3}{8}$ of 40 = 15. $40 - 8 - 10 - 15 = 7$

10. 23·865   Make sure points are in a straight column. Remember 3 = 3·0
$$\begin{array}{r} 9\cdot005 \\ 11\cdot32 \\ +\quad 3\cdot0 \\ 0\cdot54 \\ \hline 23\cdot865 \end{array}$$

11. 165 $\frac{3}{4}$ of 1100 = 825. $825 \div 5 = 165$

12. 30°   Addition of all the angles gives 12w. $w = 360° \div 12 = 30°$

13. (a) 2924
$$\begin{array}{r} 86 \\ \times\quad 34 \\ \hline 344 \\ 258\mathbf{0} \\ \hline 2924 \end{array}$$

    (b) 2 924 000
    (c) 2·924   3 decimal places in question, so 3 decimal places in answer 2·**924**

14. (a) 16% $\frac{4}{25} = \frac{16}{100}$

    (b)

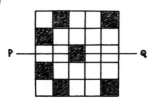

    (c) 28% $\frac{7}{20} = \frac{28}{100}$

15. (i) 2 ;   (ii) 9 ;   (iii) 64

16. 9 metres   Area of flowerbed = 6 × 6 = 36 m². Area of remaining lawn is also 36 m².
Total area is 36 + 36 = 72 m². Width of lawn is 8 m, so length is 72 m ÷ 8 = 9 m.

17. (a) $\frac{3}{8}$ Think of 4 as $3\frac{8}{8}$. $3\frac{8}{8} - 3\frac{5}{8} = \frac{3}{8}$

  (b) $\frac{1}{5}$ Lowest common denominator is 30. $\frac{25}{30} + \frac{2}{30} - \frac{21}{30} = \frac{6}{30} = \frac{1}{5}$

18. (a) KA$26.60   (b) £300

19. 0

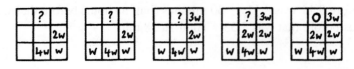

20. −3·2°C   8·5 − 5·3 = 3·2 , so 5·3 − 8·5 = −3·2

21. (i) (8 , 7)

   (ii) , (iii)

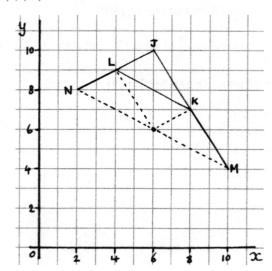

  (iv) (6 , 6)
  (v) 1 : 3

22. 29%   64 crows, 78 gulls and 58 pigeons remained. The total number of birds remaining
was 200. Pigeons made up $\frac{58}{200} = \frac{29}{100} = 29\%$ of the total number.

23. 46 square units   Area of each of the three triangles outside the black triangle can be calculated, using

the formula: area of triangle = $\frac{\text{base} \times \text{height}}{2}$

Total area of the three triangles is 24 + 20 + 10 = 54 square units.
Area of black triangle is 100 − 54 = 46 square units.

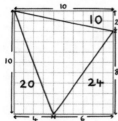

24. 1011 mb

Average for 7 days was 1005 × 7 = 7035

Total recorded on 6 days, apart from Saturday, was 6024.   7035 − 6024 = 1011

25. (a) 5998
+ 2988
8986

In the units column, the missing digits could be 3 or 8. Although 3 would fit in the hundred, tens and units columns, it would not fit in the thousands column.

(b) 7

The result ends with 9 in the units column. The only possible multiplications to give a 9 in the units column are 333 × 33 (3 threes are **9**) or 777 × 77 (7 sevens are 4**9**). The first of these gives an answer which is too low.

26. (a) 3
(b) 13

Each of the creatures has a head, so there are 16 creatures altogether.
Dogs have 4 legs each; hens have 2 legs each.

If there is 1 dog, there are 15 hens.   There are 4 + 30 = 34 legs.
If there are 2 dogs, there are 14 hens.   There are 8 + 28 = 36 legs.
If there are **3 dogs**, there are **13 hens**.   There are 12 + 26 = **38 legs**.

(This could also be done by simultaneous equations, but would probably take longer.)

27. (a) 5.00 p.m.
(b) 9 miles

At 3.00 p.m. Layla has walked 3 miles; Victoria has walked 1 mile.
At 4.00 p.m. Layla has walked 6 miles; Victoria has walked 5 miles.
At 5.00 p.m. Layla has walked 9 miles and Victoria has also walked 9 miles

(c) 5.40 p.m.

Going at Layla's speed of 3 miles/hour, they will take another $\frac{2}{3}$ hour = 40 minutes to complete the remaining 2 miles.

28. $\frac{3}{5}$

Radius of circle is 5 cm, so diameter is 10 cm.
Length of square is also 10 cm (imagine the circle turned so that A and B touch the square).
Perimeter of △ ABC = 10 + 6 + 8 = 24 cm; perimeter of square = 4 × 10 = 40 cm.
$$\frac{24}{40} = \frac{3}{5}$$

29. (i) A: 1 , B: 3
(ii) 961
(iii) 619 and 691

Square root of 169 is 13.
Number with digits BA is 31.   31 × 31 = 961
Of the four other arrangements, two of them (196 and 916) are even numbers, so they divide by 2 and cannot be prime. This leaves only 619 and 691.

(iv) 196 is the square of 14

30. 20

Number of British passengers = 122 − 73 = 49
Number of married British passengers = 80 − 51 = 29
So number of unmarried British passengers = 49 − 29 = 20

PAPER K. Answers and explanations.

1.(a) 16, 28 — Adding 6 each time

  (b) 10, $2\frac{1}{2}$, $1\frac{1}{4}$ — Dividing by 2 each time

2. 654

3.
$$\begin{array}{r} 1749 \\ + \ 5674 \\ \hline 7423 \end{array}$$

4. 9876

5. 4213

6. 2 056 009

7. 32

If $\frac{5}{8}$ of the number = 20 , $\frac{1}{8}$ of the number = 20 ÷ 5 = 4.
The number is 4 × 8 = 32.

8. $\frac{6}{\ } = \frac{8}{12} = \frac{20}{\ } = \frac{}{18}$

Each of these fractions is equivalent to $\frac{2}{3}$

9. Q = 47° ; R = 94°

Q + R = 180 − 39 = 141° ;   141° divided by 3 = 47° ;   47° × 2 = 94°

10. 2·353

Set out columns carefully
$$\begin{array}{r} 1\cdot627 \\ - \ \ 0\cdot34 \\ \hline 1\cdot287 \\ + \ \ 1\cdot066 \\ \hline 2\cdot353 \end{array}$$

11. (a) 0·75

$3 \div 4 = 0\cdot75$ **or** $\frac{3}{4} = \frac{75}{100} = 0\cdot75$

  (b) 61%

  (c) $\frac{7}{20}$

12. 24

Multiples of 5 up to 32 are: 5 , 10 , 15 , 20 , 25 , 30
Numbers 1 less than a multiple of 5 are: 4 , 9 , 14 , 19 , 24 , 29
Two of these, 9 and 24 will divide by 3 (in 3x table).
9 is 1 more than 8 which is not a prime number.
That leaves **24** which is 1 more than prime number 23.

13. (a) 20

  (b) $\frac{3}{100}$ (or 3 hundredths)

  (c) 600

  (d) $\frac{7}{10}$ (or 7 tenths)

14. 112 cm

Mass × distance on Kathy's side = 35 × 80 = 2800
Distance of Jo on the other side = 2800 ÷ 25 = 112

15. (a) $\frac{9}{10}$

Lowest common denominator is 20. $\quad \frac{15}{20} + \frac{7}{20} - \frac{4}{20} = \frac{18}{20} = \frac{9}{10}$

(b) $3\frac{3}{4}$

Change mixed numbers to improper fractions:

$$1\frac{4}{11} \times \frac{2}{3} \times 4\frac{1}{8} = \frac{15}{11} \times \frac{2}{3} \times \frac{33}{8} \ . \quad \text{Then} \quad \frac{5}{1} \times \frac{1}{1} \times \frac{3}{4} = \frac{15}{4} = 3\frac{3}{4}$$

16. (a) 11

11 occurs more times than any other number.

(b) 12

When the numbers are placed in order of size, 12 is in the middle.

$\qquad$ 9 , 10 , 11 , 11 , 11 , **12** , 13 , 14 , 14 , 19 , 19

(c) 13

Total ages 143 ; number of people 11 . Mean = 143 ÷ 11 = 13

17. 12 cm²

Perimeter of large rectangle is 44 cm, so width is 16 cm (16 + 6 + 16 + 6 = 44).
Area of large rectangle = 16 × 6 = 96 cm².
Area of small rectangle = $\frac{1}{4}$ × area of large rectangle = 24 cm²
Area of shaded triangle = 24 ÷ 2 = 12 cm²

This can be seen better if the figures inside the large rectangle are moved to the left:

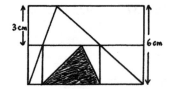 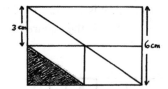

18. [a] 20

Work out then bracket first (8 − 3) = 5

[b] 32

Multiplication and division before addition and subtraction 2 + 30

[c] 15

Multiplication first 7 × 3 = 21. Then 4 + 21 = 25. 25 − 10 = 15

[d] 6

Brackets first (11 − 8) = 3.

19. 38 and 23

The larger of the two numbers is the mean (average) of 61 and 15 = $\frac{61+15}{2}$ = 38

_or_ by trial and error starting at 31 and 30 (difference = 1), 32 and 29 (difference = 3), etc.

20. (a) −4
(b) 42
(c) 53

21. (a) 54°

15% of 360 = 54

(b) 600 g

25% is $\frac{1}{4}$ of the cake, so the whole cake is 150 g × 4 = 600 g

(c) 10%

Sugar and butter make up 100 − 40 − 25 − 15 = 20%, so 10% of the cake is butter.

(d) 240 g

40% of 600 g = 240 g

22. 16

Volume of cuboid = length × width × height.
Volume of tank A = 24 × 12 × y ; volume of tank B = y × y × 18
Tank volumes are equal so 24 × 12 × y = y × y × 18
Dividing both sides of the equation by y, you get 288 = 18y.   y = 288 ÷ 18 = 16

23. 54°   Each of the five angles in the centre is 360 ÷ 5 = 72° (all the way round is 360°).
The pentagon is regular, so Δ BOC is isosceles.   180 – 72 = 108° shared equally
between the other two angles in the Δ .   108 ÷ 2 = 54°

24. (a) 100 000   100 cm = 1 m ; 1 000 m = 1 km ;   100 x 1000 = 100 000
(b) 2·2 km   11 x 20 000 = 220 000 cm = 2·2 km
(c) 15 cm   3 km = 300 000 cm ;   300 000 cm ÷ 20 000 = 15 cm

25. 125%   If B is 100, 20 (or 20%) has to be subtracted to make 80.
If A is 80, 20 has to be added to make 100.   20 is 25% of 80, so B is 125% of A.

26. A (36 , 0)   The x coordinate of M is 18, so the x coordinate of A is 18 x 2 = 36. A lies on the x
axis so its y coordinate is 0.
C (9 , 18)   The y coordinate of M is 12, so the y coordinate of B is 12 x 2 = 24.
C is half-way between M (18 , 12) and B (0 , 24) which is (9 , 18).

27. (a) 4   77 x 2 = 154 (not enough) ; 77 x 3 = 231 (not enough) ; 77 x 4 = 308
(b) 3 d-deckers and 4 minibuses   3 double-deckers (231 people) + 4 minibuses (64 people) = 295

28. (a) 529 and 952
(b) 295 and 925
(c) 37   259 is 7 x **37** ;   592 is 16 x **37** ;   925 is 25 x **37**
(d) 529   529 is the square of 23

29.

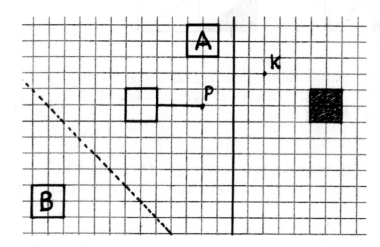

30. 60   If you know how to do simultaneous equations, this is quite easy but, if not, try (perhaps)
100 children. This gives a total amount of (131x12) + (100x7) = £2 272.
Not enough, so there must be more than 131 adults and fewer than 100 children.
Try (perhaps) 90 children or 80 children and see how the totals change.